AF266938

THE BIOGRAPHER

POEMS

DAVID M. KATZ

DOS MADRES

2024

DOS MADRES PRESS INC.

P.O. Box 294, Loveland, Ohio 45140

www.dosmadres.com   editor@dosmadres.com

Dos Madres is dedicated to the belief that the small press is essential to the vitality of contemporary literature as a carrier of the new voice, as well as the older, sometimes forgotten voices of the past. And in an ever more virtual world, to the creation of fine books pleasing to the eye and hand.

Dos Madres is named in honor of Vera Murphy and Libbie Hughes, the "Dos Madres" whose contributions have made this press possible.

Dos Madres Press, Inc. is an Ohio Not For Profit Corporation and a 501 (c) (3) qualified public charity. Contributions are tax deductible.

Executive Editor: Robert J. Murphy

Illustration & Book Design: Elizabeth H. Murphy
www.illusionstudios.net

Typeset in Adobe Garamond Pro & Bell MT
ISBN 978-1-962847-07-0
Library of Congress Control Number: 2024934087

First Edition

Published by Dos Madres Press, Inc.

ACKNOWLEDGEMENTS

I'm grateful to the editors of these publications for first accepting and publishing the following poems, some of which have been revised.

Able Muse: "The Real Hart Crane"

Alabama Literary Review: "Tea with Cavafy," "Seventies Rejection Note," "Legend Must Do"

BigCityLit: "To the Age"

Birmingham Poetry Review: "The Young Philatelist," "A Trickle of Warmth" (forthcoming)

The Classical Outlook: "Glyconics at Bryn Mawr"

The Ekphrastic Review: "Miró's Intention"

Poetry In Performance: "Epiphany" (originally "Interlude")

The Raintown Review: "Are You Still Drinking, Dad?" (forthcoming)

The Solitary Plover: "In the Condensery"

Cover: Photograph of "The Table (Still Life with Rabbit)" by Joan Miró (Spain), 1920-1921.

Other Photographs: Lower East Side pushcart market 1908-1916, Library of Congress.

For my family

CONTENTS

THE BIOGRAPHER

THE BIOGRAPHER

To the Age

There are so many things you do not like
But cannot change yourself. You are a mule
That will not leave its stall. Your hollows ache.
You're never what you are. You are no fool,
But neither are you smart. You make demands,
You dictate how we talk about ourselves,
Supply material for our labels, brands,
And dirty jokes, the canned goods on our shelves.
We've taken you for jazz and innocence,
Things that change, although you stay the same
For all the time you're here. You make no sense
Except to stand for our collective shame.
We each pass through you like the stagnant air,
A darkened cloud, this toxic atmosphere.

LEGEND MUST DO

His Last Book

It had a slapdash quality, assembled
In haste as it was, the poet's intimations
Of mortality assaulting him
In droves that summer when he realized
He was no longer young. He recognized
A periodic feebleness of mind,
A lack of balance, tendency to slip
And wobble in his steps, rise in the night
Repeatedly to pee: Of scant concern
In themselves, these irksome little symptoms,
Annoying as mosquito bites,
Together made it seem to him as if
There were just two things in the universe
That mattered: his life and the end of it,
And the end of it was closing in on life
Like a wall, as if a wall could start to walk
With sure intention toward another wall,
The poet's life the gap between the walls,
A gap diminishing with greater speed
These last few weeks, or so he had imagined.
And so he wrote and jettisoned excess,
Injecting life in poems long thought dead,
Sorting out survivors on the floor.
The season waned, but not the August heat,
And there were days he ached to quit the book
And catch the sun before it headed down
Into the energetic, steel-gray sea.
Yet every time he felt the urge to flee
His need to be remembered beat it back
Like an overwhelming wave. Lashed to his desk,
Fearing death, he forced the poems out.

The Real Hart Crane

The bottom of the sea is cruel.
—Hart Crane, "Voyages"

The only evidence we have is clear:
Hart Crane was never who we thought he was.
The sum of him's a bridge carved out of air,
North Labrador, the Keys, the Southern Cross,
Stations of an aspiration blue
As the empyrean. He's not someone
We lost at sea in 1932.

Yet that's the man we fix our focus on.
He breathed his last just shy of thirty-three,
And then was made a martyr to his art.
The agonies of his biography,
The lurid ways in which he fell apart,
Deflect us from the lexicon he is,
The only part of him that surfaces.

The Old Neighborhood

Today I thought I'd visit you again.
Pastrami sandwiches in Tompkins Square:
Everything the same as it was then.

As I recall, I'd take the southbound train.
Grand Street would be the stop to get me there.
Today I thought I'd visit you again.

I ran away from home when I was ten
And found in you my native atmosphere.
Everything would be the same as then,

Babushkas roasting yams and stirring brine,
Their Yiddish thickening the smoky air.
Today I thought I'd visit you again.

I thought I could relive the moment when
I tasted pickled fish beyond compare.
But not a thing's the same as it was then,

The elders of your avenues complain.
The realtors have brought them to despair.
Today I thought I'd visit you again,
And everything would be the same as then.

The Bear Who Comes to You in Dreams

The heavy bear who goes with me
—-Delmore Schwartz

The bear who comes to you in dreams
Is on the hunt for something wild,
For anything but you. His snout
Aloft above the traffic, he
Indulges in a dullish side-
Long glance. He sees you cowering
Against a chain-link schoolyard fence.
He passes by without a sound
And goes on his appointed round.
You slip into your morning shadow
Like a sleeping bag upon a meadow
And drift to deeper sleep again.
But clouds are passing, countless sheep
Are milling, massing to depart.
You've now become a silver fish
Flapping on a sidewalk, chum
Alluring to a famished bear.
Hide, you dream, although you lack
A hiding place. *Play dead*, you rasp,
But your fins will not be stilled. *Accept*.
You toss, and he's a circus bear
On a unicycle, parasol
Between his paws. It's begun to rain.
A wheel is rolling to a stop.
You hear the bear's umbrella drop.
His heart is pounding in your dreams.

Legend Must Do

I was born on the Lower East Side of New York
To shopkeepers just off the boat from Galitz
In the Russian Pale. My grandpa's wrapped
In a story now, in the wooliness of legend.
Among the men we have woven into
A generation, he was drafted into the army
Of the Czar. His palooka of a sergeant
Was easy game, and grandpa took a pint
Of vodka out and got the sergeant drunk.
Weaving along the side of a ditch
In a dizzy march, the two moved on,
The officer fell in, and my grandpa deserted
Into the woods. I have no idea
Whether any of this is true, but
Legend must do when the facts are few.
My grandpa had an accent, opened up
A tailor shop, was father to my mother
And her sister (a Communist! "Milk
For babies!" she shouted for the poor).
That's all I remember except for the lumpy vests,
The slight white frame, the scar of the appendectomy
He revealed to me, shaving by the frigid toilet.
"They cut out half my stomach, boychick."
He smoked Phillies and died when I was eight.

The Altitude

I walked beside my father's giant leg,
Hip-high, no more than five. His head and hat
Were in the sky. Suddenly I pitched
Forward like a ship, the mica chips
In concrete hurtling up at me before
My arm grew taut. My father's hand had held
Me back from falling, though he didn't seem
To notice, and we took a slow next step.
My eyes rose up and saw, beneath his hat,
A jaw, a nose, and something like a smile.
There may have been a raincoat and some rain.
Behind this scene, upon this screen, I see
The start of all I've come to think of him,
The New York City street surrounding us,
The fences and gray spaces, autumn rain,
The firmness of his hand, the altitude
I'd have to climb before I knew the man.

A Prayer for Gerald Ford

The persistent phrase applied to Gerald Ford
Is that he never could chew gum and walk
At the same time. I recall his great bald head
Ardently raised, the pages of a speech
Falling from his arm, his eyes aloft
As if unto the heavens, tripping forward
On the first step while ascending toward
The podium. I've always found this odd,
Since Ford had been a running back, a role
Requiring a sense of balance, yet
He was also known to stumble *off*
The dais when completing an address.
I've always sympathized with Gerald Ford
Since I am cut from the same ungainly cloth.
When I was young, transfixed by comic books,
By baseball, poetry, and girls, I banged
Into walls, skinned my knees and tore my pants,
Bruised my skull on open cupboard doors,
Which to this day I always fail to close.
And yet often, sitting in a synagogue,
My mind asleep mid-sermon, I have stirred
Awake when the rabbi paused to ask the same
Rhetorical question: "How can it be
That our lives amount to dust and ashes
Even though our faces radiate
The aura of the Lord?" I thus declare
That clumsiness is next to godliness
And pray that Gerald Ford will be redeemed,
And that there still might be some hope for me.

"For the Love of God, Montressor"

I recall the roughness
>of my father's cheek
As he paged through
>Poe's *Collected Works*
As he had before,
>discovering again,
As if spontaneously,
>"The Cask of Amontillado."
I recall the tightening
>of his grip
Around my ribs,
>his whisper threatening
From the last words
>of the very first sentence:
"I vowed revenge."
>I feared for Fortunato,
His foolish cap and bells,
>his clownish
Helplessness.
>I feared
The hearty handshake
>hiding
The malice
>of Montressor
And the familiar
>scent of whiskey
On my father's breath.

*

Down we climbed
            through the icy
                        catacombs,
Our fingers twirling
            the nitrous webs'
                        cat's cradle,
The skulls watching
            as he read, and we
                        descended.
If my father
            was Montressor,
                        the secret oppressor,
I must have been
            Fortunato,
                        the silly jester
Inattentive
            to his fate, or
                        were we,
Are we,
            interchangeable
                        to this date,

The last brick
            in the wall
                        about to smother us?

"For the love of God,
            Montressor!"

The Death of Akiva

Before my final disobedience,
Before the rabbi kicked me out of school,
He would take off his glasses, rub his eyes,
Pull down a book of Jewish history,
Legends mostly, sigh, and seem to say,
I'm tired of fighting, tired of all the rules.
Let us be together now. One day
He read to us about Akiva's death.
"When Rome had banned the study of Torah,
Akiva, first among the sages, still
Convened assemblies in the public square
To delve into the mysteries of God."
An image that remains with me today
Is of the armored Romans stoning him
And of Akiva dying slowly, stone
After stone, and calling out to Israel
That the Lord is one, *echad*, a final cry
To singularity before he fell.
To this day, I whisper to myself
Akiva's final words before I fall asleep,
A stay against the fear of being swept
Up by the darkness. They provide for me
A way to move past my imagined sins,
Errors of omission, deeds undone,
And past the certain punishment to come.

The Person I Remember

The person I remember couldn't lie.
I was the only person on the block,
A half mile from my father's home hard by
The river. All at once three pairs of sneakers
Slapped the ground, and at my back I felt
The iron grating of a garden gate.
Chewing gum, the first guy stared at me,
Then glanced away in nonchalance, or feigned
Nonchalance, at the streetlamps blinking on,
The pavement, and the darkening sky above
New Jersey. The coast is clear, he might have thought,
Turning to regard the person I remember,
The one who couldn't lie. "You Jew?" he asked,
Seeming to know the answer he would get,
Not that it would have made a difference.
The person that I was sensed time slow down
As if to help me find the right reply
To the question. Was I, then, a Jew?
If I was, I'd have to answer yes,
For that was in the nature of the thing
Itself: to own up to the fact on pain
Of death, or, in this case, of being punched
In the face, thrown to the ground, and kicked
Senseless. Nonetheless, I answered yes.
"Too bad," that first guy said. He hit me hard.
I had to take a swing to stay alive.
I caught him with a long one on the cheek
And clipped the other two. The sky was dark.
I was the only person on the block.
The person I remember couldn't lie.

Ignis Fatuus

> *ignis fatuus*: a light that sometimes appears in the night over
> marshy ground
> —Merriam-Webster

> Better an ignis fatuus
> Than no illume at all
> —Emily Dickinson

To my sister

Although your tumor isn't cancerous,
The surgery entails a certain risk.
I'm in New York. You're in Los Angeles.
A distance that has meant paralysis
Assumes a different emphasis.

Certainly I'll call; I often have.
I'm your big brother, one on whom you count
For the minimal and temporary salve
Of a birthday conversation. To be blunt:
You aren't here, and I am distant.

Our different fathers hover in the wings,
Hiding who was mine and who was yours.
Offstage, our mother had maternal flings;
We're left to weigh the facts against the source
And let the drama take its course.

The characters assume a certain fit.
Two had slick hair. The lawful one was bald,
The pop we lived with years before they split,
The one who asked me why you hadn't called
And dubbed me his "beloved" child

Though I was born a bastard of his wife
The same as you. She stopped at any mirror
To fix her face, fashion us a life,
And rinse her hair in amorous water.
From coast to coast, electric star

Of the show, she rises on the telephone
Between us in her fifties evening dress.
Her J&B, her cigarettes, cologne
Complete the portrait of her vast success
At staying young and glamorous.

We smell and hear her, even start to see her
Vanish down the hall and shut the door,
A hat-check girl who worked the Latin Quarter
To find herself another ardent suitor
And an adequate provider.

Vanishing, an ignis fatuus,
She left with us for Vegas on a red-eye—
With us, but already fading from us.
In our illumined cabin in the sky
We saw a grown-up woman fly.

In front of us, dear sister, in the dark,
A phosphorescence slips across a swamp.
Its glow evokes a spirit with a spark,
A wink of mambo, meteoric vamp.
No eyes but ours can find the lamp.

The Divine Wind

There by my father's bed was *Analog*,
With Robert Heinlein, Isaac Asimov,
And others on the cover. He slept in space,
Floating in vast regions, while I watched.
Earlier, we'd read a paperback
About the kamikazes. Their routine:
So spare and clean. Awakening at dawn,
Each one put a helmet on, climbed up
Into a cockpit, plighted his allegiance
To the eternal empire, and took off.

Are You Still Drinking, Dad?

19

Are you still drinking, Dad? He wouldn't say
At first or, rather, couldn't. I'd never asked,
And he may have wondered if he'd got away
Without the need to answer for his lapse.
I thought it was a decade since he'd quit.
It might have been. He might have had one shot,
A rye to ease the future shock a bit;
Sweet Gypsy Rose; cheap peach or apricot
Liqueur. I said I'd be a father soon,
And he was miles away across the phone
On some highway with a cowboy tune
Fading behind. He always drank alone.
It's now or never, Dad, I might have said.
Before my son was born my dad was dead.

Out of the Past

You find yourself in a deserted industrial park,
The flues warped and twisted, ramps disengaged,
The smoke barely dispersed. This was a place
You once had lived, although there's little sign of life,
Little to identify the small streets, the avenues
Of your past. It's morning now, and you cough
At the cloud blocking the sun, then look for someone.
There she is, just past the back of a foundation,
Wandering like you. There are benevolent details
As you get close to them: a trickle, a rivulet
Of clear water reflecting the dawn, a ladybug.
The twisted pipes, the filters, gears, torn
Conveyor belts hanging like thick rubber bands,
The colossal sense of idleness recede. The ladybug
Is something to behold. It is morning, you are
Awakening, and the woman is walking toward you.

The Young Philatelist

Time compresses as you age, and each
Age seems a glossy stamp from Zanzibar,
The Vatican, or Monaco–ones you,
The young philatelist, would marvel at,
Turn every puckered album page, and dream
Of your escape. Perhaps you'd find yourself,
In bed in your own room when you were ten,
The minutes slowly passing by, then coming
To a halt, you gazing at the pale young queen
On the upper right-hand edge of every one
Of your British colonials. Next to your bed,
A Raleigh bicycle, and on your desk
A glue-encrusted plastic replica
Of the *Saratoga*, amply fortified
With fighter jets, artillery, a deck
Three times the length of a football field, a ship
That could defend you from attacks by air
Or sea or land. But not an atom bomb.
Your room could be your Alamo, your last
Redoubt against the sudden end of things.
You were so peaceful and so quiet there,
As unobtrusive as a postage stamp.

Birth Father

They had boarded the bus to Atlantic City
At the terminal. My sister's eyes were darting,
My mother's in a trance. It was almost three and a half hours
From the Port Authority, through the toxic air
Of Elizabeth, the patches of standing water in Raritan.
They descended into the afternoon fumes
Of their destination, an obscure casino,
Passing through revolving doors to an eatery
Outdoors on the boardwalk. I imagine they
Ordered the shrimp and avocado salad.
                                        And there
He was, approaching lightly from the farthest corner,
Weaving through the labyrinth of tables, his entire being
The widening gleam of a smile. Our mother offered her cheek,
And he engulfed her fragile frame. "This is Harry.
I think I mentioned him to you." Before the salads
Arrived, she whispered to my sister that the specter
With the shiny silver hair was her birth father.
Father and daughter glanced into each other's eyes; nothing
Was revealed; and in a quarter of an hour he vanished
Into the air from whence he came. The salads may have been
Indifferently consumed, the water drunk. But that is immaterial,
As are the weightless words that passed between them
And the air, heavy with fumes, at the Atlantic City station.

A Trickle of Warmth

"Only one can of Beacon Wax the whole day."
It was a slender taking for my old man,
Sitting there in Spanish Harlem in his cold
Linoleum store. They also called it oilcloth,
But whatever they called it, not one roll
Of it had left the store that hard December.
Fathers and mothers were preferring carpeting
From companies like Mohawk, and the small churches
Could no longer pay to heal their injured floors,
Another staple of the business. He came home frozen
On the outside and the inside, immobile
In the dingy flannel shirt that he had worn
For days. He brought the cold inside, or else the cold
Greeted him at the open door as he stomped his feet
On the wordless welcome mat. Although my memory
Has never allowed a trickle of warmth to pass between them,
I now can grant my mother might have greeted him
With a whispered mention of his name as she turned
From the oval mirror, and he might have done the same,
Her name escaping in the softest hiss from the side
Of his mouth. There were signs of affection in the letters
They exchanged when he was stationed down in Little Rock
And she was in New York, and in a photo of her sitting
In his lap and one in a wheelbarrow as he stood behind her,
Smiling in his starched khakis. That I never
Saw them like that doesn't mean they never were
In love. It only means I was too young to see it.

Private Joke

"They burn me up," the caption read. Unfolding
The sepia tabloid cartoon for me
As she had many times before, grandma,
Elegant though she was, pronounced the verb
"Boin." She pointed first to FDR,
His long cape slung across his ailing shoulders,
Cigarette in holder tight between teeth
Clenched into a rictus, a squiggle of smoke
Rising into the air. Next was Churchill,
Slunk down, his homburg just above his brows,
The ever-present stogie butt ejecting
Billows. Last was Stalin, with his calabash
And Magritte moustache, venting vortices
Of vapor. Together, their exhaust assaulted
A little Hitler scrunched down in the left
Corner, his perfect circle of a mouth
Coughing. "They boin me up," my grandma laughed,
As if their war had been our private joke.

Tea with Cavafy

People think of me—
I would have them think of me—
As a poet, without qualification, as I
Attested by stating that as my occupation
On my passport. There's a difference, though,
Between that face and who I truly am,
Between my tortoise shells and homeliness
In three-quarter profile and the words
That are speaking with you here and now.
Note my faded window screen, the ghosts
Of my city in its weave of fleur-de-lis.
It allows me to sleep, but also enables
The light to caress my spirit at dawn.
I have moved the screen aside, drawn
The heavy drapes to admit the glow,
Like the moon that pulls the waves away
In front of a porthole. Simply stated,
That muted glow is who I truly am,
And who I truly am, you may imagine,
Is a man sitting quietly in his study,
Enabling each thought, each image,
Each word to emerge slowly, arising
Between you and me, gentle visitor.
Out of the glow, black letters of a phrase
Will settle in your mind as if they came
Directly from my living lips, conjuring
A lover I was yearning then to see
For a few fateful moments one afternoon
When I was in despair of losing him.
Though he is gone, my words are here for you,
As present as this heated pot of tea.

Second Sight

Two times you ask us if we've seen the work
You've done this sunny afternoon in May,
A book of pencil sketches of the park
Viewed from a bench. Unsure of what to say,
We answer you again. We cross with you
On Riverside, not far from where we live
Just blocks apart on West End Avenue.
You've never seen a light like this: the drive
Dimmed by buildings, intermittent trees,
And passing clouds that only emphasize
Precise illumination. Your eyes seize
That, and only that, and through your eyes
We realize how much you still can see,
How light survives your loss of memory.

In the Condensery

Lorine Niedecker wrote about water,
How it buckled the wooden floor
Of their cottage in Wisconsin—
On Blackhawk Island, to be
Precise, as she was—her father
A carp fisherman, her mother going
Deaf, presumably inattentive,
Providing the girl with many
Silent hours to condense the
Things she saw into "milk,"
"Fish," broad generic words
Which could suffice for the
Watery green of her girlhood,
No names necessary. As she grew
She saw her trade as working
In a "condensery," which was
Her word for where she would
Silently boil and sweeten
Her given pint of language
And condense her father's catch.

Epiphany

I learned from Joyce the name of certain times,
Havens held until they disappear
Into the mind and outer world the mind
Surrounds, that peaceful place (is it a place?)
Where who you are, must try to do and be,
Pours through you with the utmost clarity:
Epiphany. I learned from Ezra Pound
About that instant when the world's stripped down
To one essential scene, in which the gods
Return to where you are, your one true home.

From myself I learned that this true home,
In this green space (in just one tree, perhaps),
Was a nest that I could build if I first named
What and who might fill it in, what boys
And girls in the green of Never Never Land,
Clinging to each other as they wait
For Peter Pan. In such an interlude,
A pause between the major scenes and sounds,
A time before my mother called me in,
I found the spot a poem might begin.

Seventies Rejection Note

It will be many years before
this poem will mean anything
to anybody. He wrote that,
And only that, in a garbled hand,
On paper with a deckled edge.
So it's a visionary poem,
I first thought, to shield myself
From hurt. It's praise for entering
The avant-garde, since I'd composed
A letter to the future from
That sorrow of a year, honoring
A poet we admired who had
Just died, half-starved, of laryngeal
Cancer, coughing from Gauloises
And funneling pints of Pernod
Down his gullet, much too young,
Yet old enough to be my father.
My second thought about the note
Seems closer to reality:
The editor had placed a curse
On me for all eternity,
Had thrown my modest elegy
Down like a detested hat
And jumped on it repeatedly.
Young though I was, I could laugh,
When I'd cooled off, at how absolute,
How Delphic his dismissal was.
I've dined out on the tale until
Today. He died two days ago,
And as I scan his swollen verse

And the eulogies of sycophants
With debts to him outstanding, see
An excess of causticity
In the tone of all the prose he wrote,
I know that he would never get
The jokes I tell about that note.

The Code

i.m. John le Carré

They were muttering in half-understood languages,
Half-wanting to be known, half-wanting to know,
Half not and half not. They were in the lobby,
Exchanging the code, partly overheard, the bellhops
Inured to it by now as they hustled
To the ever-ringing bell in their tight red coats
In the grandly named hotel—
Grandly named but named so many times
It had lost all but a smidgen of its grandeur.
Was the code tapped out in their syllables?
Everyone faintly wondered, even the spies
Themselves as they tried to work out what it was
They were assigned to do, even though
They were mostly on their own, or at least partly so.
The code was fading, that much was certain,
Like the paint on a repairman's shack
In a long-forgotten duchy. The honor of the code,
The honor of the service, those were surely things
That were part of long ago, the outer trappings
Faded now, but the intended meanings too.

Bashō Attempts a Sestina

Damn! This is hard work:
    six stanzas for their money.
Haikus are my life:
my food, clothing, sex.
    But Italian poetry
is now on order.

They place the order,
    and I put my verse to work
to make poetry.
I have no money,
    live alone, and have no sex.
Mountains are my life.

Rivers surge with life.
    My life maintains its order
Without any sex.
My love is my work—
    my lady's love was money,
never poetry.

Haiku poetry
    has been my source of life,
Not food or money.
Sestinas order
    my poor words to overwork.
Six can equal sex

in Latin, and sex
    appears in French poetry
more often than work.
Can I bring new life
    to this alien order?
I *am* in need of money.

Yet besides money
    and better prospects for sex,
this six-word order
in my poetry
    seems to have brought me to life
and life to my work.

Thus order, money,
    hard work, and adequate sex
give poetry life.

This poem came about after the poets Moira Egan and John Foy challenged each other and other poets to write a sestina using these end words: "work," "money," "life," "sex," "poetry," and "order."

Linseed Oil

> Used linseed oil and later that of mink.
> And always kept a ball in it
> —Robert Murphy

It's sad how kids attach themselves to things
And the things retain a life, a simulacrum,
As if the past were actual and could
Be carried with them, staying as they are
Forever. Linseed oil was what I used
To keep my Wilson outfield mitt as soft
And flexible as it would need to be
For me to catch a Major League fly ball.
I pray the leather's held that pungent smell,
More olive oil than gasoline, and much
More faint, and that it's somehow still alive,
On some kid's hand, though it's been sixty years
Since it protected mine in deep right field.

You Must Change Your Life

Accept the task that comes to you
By mule and horseback, by oxcart
And truck, from merchants pouring out
Plenty. It comes from far away,
Or near at hand, or somewhere in
Between. No matter: Change is there
Before you on the green crepe table.
Haul in the dice, the billiard balls.
Pick up your cue, and play it through.

Mirror Cells

I've lived entire lives in narrow rooms,
But now see something else entirely–
An undivided field of yellow grain.
A few tall stalks, bent back by wind, have left
A path for me to see you as you really are,
Someone like me in some respects, in others
Someone else, scratching her own itch,
Distressed by thoughts that I could never grasp
The way you do because I lack the spark
Of being you. Yet I can empathize,
I really can, for while I watch you read,
Then pause and seem to think, turn up the light,
Small rooms inside my brain, the theory goes,
Are mirroring the finest grains of all
You do, and moving me to feel that I
Can do it too: pick up the book, turn on
The light, and turn it up to make it bright.

Glyconics at Bryn Mawr

Marianne exceedingly loved
Doctor Sanders' accolade:
"interchangeably man and fish,"
Her description of Caliban
In her poem "Ennui," could rank,
Metrically, among the Greeks'.
Modesty itself, Miss Moore
Said that she had no hard and fast
Grasp of what it was she'd done,
Wrote her mother that she felt
Like a mouse on a high chair
Squeaking Dionysian hymns.

Marianne's Ox

She fakes, goes in one direction
on the matter of the buffalo–
                        American?
                That faded, lost, melancholic
                        icon of extinction–
the white mystical
                mound,

the white buffalo of television,
the long-gone ghost of a bison
                        hallucinated by Rusty,
                the cavalry boy
                        on *Rin Tin Tin*—
the name of the blessèd
                shepherd comforting him—

I say she fakes in
that direction, merely
                by being American,
                feints and catalogs
                categories of oxen—
from "the great extinct wild aurochs"
                        to Hereford, to Holstein.

"Not this and then not that,
in nothing we begin."
                        Methodically paring
                        Creation away, the author
                        of the Rg Veda
parallels Marianne
                        and Occam,

beginning only at the turn
of the beginning. Not the sad
                                American bison, but the "albino-
                                footed" Indian water
                                buffalo serves
the Buddha, the
                        job that must be done

before the setting of the sun. Marianne's
ox is a thing of use, but does
                                not do what you
                        expect it to
                                because it is as unpredictable
as the human whose hay
                        it is hauling to market.

Miró's Intention

To get to that space where the world falls away,
The canvas stares at the viewer like arrows

> While the viewer stares like a target.
> It is the painting looking at you.

That specific painting, looking at just you.
At the top of the table, there's a rooster.

> The rooster, live, uncooked, in Catalan.
> Look at the living fish, on a plate in Spain.

In a Spain no viewer has ever been,
A plant-like mother is the nation's anchor,

> A fish-like father is the nation's water.
> A beautiful bird reveals the unknown,

Reveals the unknown to a pair of lovers—
An unseen bird, as the world falls away.

THE BIOGRAPHER

The Biographer

A Verse Novella

To Marianne Moore

The biographer needs…to admit her own uncertainty and
ambivalence, and the best way to do that is to make that biographer…into
an essential part of the work itself. You guard against your own creeping
subjectivity by embracing it.
—"Having the Last Word," Michael Gorra,
The New York Review of Books, March 9, 2023

1. The Pinwheel

I always begin with a past, although
      here in America the past is always
                  problematic.
      If the origin of a grandparent
               is vague,
      as it must be for an immigrant
                 borne
on a ship in 1914
            or from below
the border in 2024,
          I must go
      back to the region of origin
              though that may go
back only one generation.

For the person I am contemplating
        for my next life study the problem is not
                                so much where she
        was born, for that, in her case, is
                                unknowable,
        foundling that she was, "lost soul of the
                                ship,"
        as the ones who thought they knew her
                                came to call her.
        No, to portray her as she really
                                might have been,
        her biographer would have to show
                                how she could change
at any given moment, how

when she walked the streets of Toledo or
        basked beneath the sun in San Francisco
                                or Laredo
        or fled from the confines of a claustral
                                city
        to the country home of a newly
                                found
        aunt she had discovered during
                                one of many
        futile searches for her ancestry,
                                how when she
        seemed most fixed, in actuality
                                she could change most
readily into someone else

entirely, how her changeableness
          distorted the view of anyone who
                              might have known her,
          anyone who might prove to be a source
                              for me.
          These photographs of her (and of me),
                              packed
          with detail, bountiful in
                              both black and white
          and color, brilliant digitals, dim
                              Polaroids
          snapped in the 1960s–from these
                              I might begin
     to still her kaleidoscopic

nature. Here *I* am, for instance, captured
          with both little feet in the air,
                              being diapered,
          my mouth zeroing in on a blood curd-
                              ling howl
          in lurid Kodachrome; beneath it,
                              there
          she is in a Dalí mustache
                              and striped polo
          in her mid-teens, a strange foreknowledge
                              in her eyes
          as if she saw what her life would be
                              if she pursued
the life of a bohemian.

In the third photograph of the pile I'm
        thumbing through, she is the very picture of
                                an odalisque,
        the full front of her body visible
                                beneath
translucent scarves. Her inscrutable
                                smile
opaque. Speaking as a woman
                                though, I can say
she appears to me in that moment
                                utterly
beautiful in a way she knew she would
                                never appear
again. It was this transience

that was her most annoying quality,
        an elusiveness that galls me the most
                                regarding her.
        Yet even a pinwheel is rooted on
                                a stick,
        the flightiest petals start with a
                                stem,
and although they are, as she was,
                                propelled by wind
as sails are, and like boats that won't move
                                without wind,
she is without breath and at rest, an
                                inert body
awaiting a biography.

2. These Treacherous Deeps

In short, she is my late mother as I
        will try in the book to imagine her
                                now that I know
        she died just a year ago, having left
                                us first
        in the 1950s when I was
                        too
        young to remember the battered steamer
                                        trunk in the door-
        way, the black velvet fascinator
                                with the mesh
        over the eyes she snatched from my father's
                                mother's house (I've
seen a photo of grandmother

wearing it when she was a young lady),
        the hot emptiness of that August day,
                                in my father's
        anguished narration. My paucity of
                                contact
        with her confers objectivity
                        on
        me—qualifies me, I suppose,
                        to render her
        in an adequately coherent
                        life story
        despite her diverse identities:
                        landless infant;
bashful ingenue; novelist;

glamorous screen actress and director;
       advocate for the poor; anti-war; anti-
                vivisectionist;
       a namer of names, though once a Party
             member.
       Newspaper clips and Web posts amount
             to
       a multimedia collage
           abounding in
       bits of fame and notoriety
           about her—
       fragmentary, yet memorably
           sensational
enough, when gathered together,

to vivify my next biography.
       Let me embark, then, on these treacherous
                maternal deeps
       defended by a sturdy hull of fact
           and leagues
       of distance. She was born in the Pale,
            placed
       in a rattan basket below
           decks by unknown
       hands halfway through her first year of life,
             dependent
       on the kindness of strangers,
           independent
by physical necessity,

that is, a solitary infancy
        on a trans-Atlantic cargo ship bound for
                                New York City
        in that fateful year of 1914.
                                Nameless
        infant in a pink blanket with the
                                Star
        of David embroidered in blue,
                                maybe by a
        mother under threat pressed to leave her
                                forever,
        liminal thing, resented object
                                of my project,
what can I possibly know of you?

3. You, Miriam Abramson

You left from Liverpool. This I can know
        of you, Miriam Abramson, abandoned
                                one: two battered
        Jews in steerage had given you their name:
                                "Abram,"
        a father of a surname and
                                "son"
        tacked on in hopes for the future.
                                This I have learned
        from the manifest: the name I came
                                to know you by,
        one of many, but an anchor
                                for your story:
"Miriam Abramson, origin

unknown. Infant found RMS *Cedric*.
Landed Ellis Island. Adopted ship-
board, Abramson
family, Shmuel and Ida, Lemberg,
Poland."
Shmuel had also clutched a fragment
of
foolscap (which I found as a child),
directing them
in Yiddish to head for Chicago,
a place where
friends might be, *lantzmen* from the old
country, tailors
and butchers and jewelers who might

employ Shmuel, greet Ida and little
Miriam into the New World. The New
World! Yet as thick
with expectation as their language was,
it could
never have caught the disorienting
swirl
when they disembarked from the train
to the platform
at Central Station, the ground
unsteady
beneath the couple's feet, the infant
in Ida's arms
shielded yet fully absorbing

the trembling concatenation, assault
        of event and sensation, recollection
                                of "the booming,
        buzzing madness" enveloping her birth.
                                Maybe
        Miriam never got over the
                        shock,
        the unceasing vibration of
                        immigration,
        a cellular uncertainty
                        handed down
        to me incessantly until I'd
                        begun to grasp
my own animus toward her.

4. Thousands of Buttons

She'd vanished in the Windy City at
        the age of ten, disappeared, her parents said,
                                in a second,
        got lost in the crowd at the Maxwell Street
                        Market,
        "our little girl lost forever," they
                        wept
        to the cops that mournful Sunday,
                                I have learned from
        puckered police logs for the summer
                        of 19
        24. Adoptive parents in
                        an adopted
country. It hadn't fared so well

for Ida and Shmuel: a tenement
      apartment in the shadow of the L, a
                        corner for a
      bassinet for the baby, hotplate,
                  outhouse
in the back. Uncle Louie, really
                not
      related, but a big shot in
                  the neighborhood,
      rented one of his pushcarts at a
                "discount" to
      the hungry couple, introduced them
                  to the notions
business, sold them strips of buttons,

needles, thread, collar stays, seam rippers,
      zippers, a panoply of accessories
                for the tailor,
      haberdasher, wholesaler, homemaker
                to hang
      on display in the Adamson cart.
                Bleak
      as business was through every week
                (Shmuel's shoulder,
      Sisyphean, pushing through the streets),
                on Sunday's
      take they could pay their bills and eat
                some kreplach soup
after the market was closed. That

was what Shmuel was dreaming of
          as the long day was winding down: Ida's
                                        original broth,
          her thin, rolled noodles, the boiled skin of
                                        the week's
          chicken. The bright sprig of parsley top-
                                        ping
          it off. He stared at his wife's hands
                                        as they neatened up
          the late-day disorder of the cart,
                                        straightening
          the sewing hooks, little scissors,
                                        the pink and red-
tomato pin cushions she'd stitched

throughout the week. While Shmuel gazed, Ida
          longed desperately to be off her feet. Their
                                        internal lives
          are of course, my own creation, as is
                                        the bulk
          of any biography, a story
                                        based
          on a handful of facts. I have seen,
                                        in fact, a creased,
          anonymous photo of a pushcart
                                        from that time
          with a grimfaced father, mother, and
                                        little girl posed
in front of it, only the name

"Chicago" discernible on the back.
       They could have been the Abramsons, could have been
                                             them or any-
       one, but to me they have become the stuff
                                    my dreams
       are made of, my madeleine of fact,
                              my
       way of making sense of the loss
                        of Miriam
       on that day a century ago.
                         In my mind
       I see her mesmerized by the sheer
                            number and
variety of buttons gathered

in the bottom of the cart—thousands, it
       might have seemed to little Miriam as she
                                    started pouring
       bunches of them from hand to hand, letting
                                    them drop
       like waterfalls to the cart, swishing
                           them
       like hockey pucks across the ice. When
                              she stopped to stare
       at a handful of them, they mingled
                           to become
       the source of every color, every
                        tone and texture
underneath the now setting sun.

Infinitudes of prismatic color!
        Deep purple, chartreuse, puce, big translucent ones
                                        for winter coats,
        tiny cream ones for the necks of dresses,
                                        painted
        wooden cameos, paisleys, fake turquoise
                                        gems
        reflecting the fire of the
                                late-setting sun
        into the wide eyes of Miriam
                                        (who always
        would have a weakness for hypnosis
                                        by means of light).
She found herself in the shadows

and did not cry out. I see her losing
        herself half-willingly, half unconsciously
                                        amid the crowd,
        driven to blend into it by a force
                                she would
        never understand, one that also
                                drove
        her to flee to a singular
                                sense of herself:
        to be part of the crowd but be
                                apart from
        the crowd: a singularity in
                                the whirlwind. *Here*
I must swallow the snake of my

creeping subjectivity. I've amassed
certain facts, images imaginary
and passingly
real. I can say I knew her as a girl
might know
a mother ever elsewhere from where
her
daughter was, always on the way
out, forever
abandoning her. I shiver to
write it, I
shivered then, when I was ten, the same
age that she was
when she first fades from history.

5. "She's Not Ours"

I will step with her now into the void
of information, the vortex, the funnel,
conjuring her
final exit from the remnants of the
shtetl
in our lives, since I hereby become
my
mother, feel my way into how
it might have been
for her to walk away from Shmuel
and Ida
into the dusk of Maxwell Street. I'm
that little girl;
what am I doing, what will I

do next? All had been revealed in a fight
       the night before: I was not their birth daughter.
                                    I heard it while
       I was tucked in bed in my
                              narrow
       dark corner of our single room, heard words
                                           of
       icy separation from me
                           when they thought I
       was asleep, words of regret about me,
                                 how much I'd
       cost, even though I was not their own
                                 and now they had
so little money. "She's not ours."

"Yes." It was what I'd long suspected, but
       hearing it opened up a chasm into
                              which I spiralled
       down through the depths of the deepest sleep, lost
                                 to them
       forever. I woke as a child wakes,
                           not
       remembering what I had heard
                              the night before.
       But "She's not ours" smoldered silently
                                 underneath,
       went on burning inside me throughout
                                 that burning day,
And in a trance I slipped away.

6. Into the American Dream

She turned up that night. "Angrily pacing
      along a bank of the Chicago River,
                        spitting, kicking
      gravel in an abandoned lumberyard,
                   a girl,
      aged ten, claiming to be an orphan with
                          no
      immediate family, was picked up
                  by the police,"
      according to the annals of an
                    immigrant
      aid society, which, to her good
                fortune, placed her
with a middle-class family,

first with her given name, then with Mary
      Evans to suit the assimilationist
                tendencies of
      Charles (Chaim) Evans (Eisenberg), her new
                  father,
      and Brenda (née Branya Blumenstein),
               her
      new mom. At first grudgingly,
                reluctantly,
      skeptically, only gradually
                comforted
      when she came to understand how much
                she was wanted
by that childless couple, how much

they needed this girl to illuminate
        the darkened upstairs bedroom in their row house
                                        in Rogers Park,
        as I imagine it, having only names,
                                places,
        and dates to mark the start of Act II
                                of
        her biography. "Lo, Levin
                        leaping lightens
        in eyeblink Ireland's westward welkin,"
                                James Joyce wrote,
        and I take that as my license to
                                envision an
eyeblink of my mother's northward

avian transmigration into the
        American Dream, a nest beneath the Lake
                                Michigan sky.
        Mary's teens were tough, her hair and moods a
                                furious
        snarl ensnaring combs and comforting
                                coos
        by Brenda importuning a
                        softening mood
        that never seemed to come.
                        Unbeknownst
        to Mary, however, beneath her
                        ferocity
an odd sense of comfort arose

in the smallest ways, a security
          she hadn't known at sea or in that shtetl
                              beneath the L.
          As Mary, she could sit for a moment
                                   on her
          pink wool bedspread, letting a moment
                                   pass
          without a thought in her head, learning
                                   for the first time
          how to daydream, a luxury she
                                   hadn't known
          while Shmuel and Ida battled
                              in front of her,
angry and hungry, hadn't known

as she plied the thousand trying tasks her
          youthful flesh had been heir to, trailing behind
                                   Shmuel's cart through
          unrelenting summer and the hawk of
                                   winter
          off the lake. Here, however, was a
                                   hush
          in a warm room of her own, an
                                   unexpected
          relaxation of tension, a new
                                   sequestration
          in which a breach by Brenda knocking
                                   on her door with
a bagel and a glass of milk

might gradually be tolerated
        and even, eventually, welcomed. She
                                might be Mary
        Evans now, might step forth from the inner
                                        fictions
        I've been fabricating as her thoughts—
                                my
        own trembling inner life placed
                                inside Mary's
        image, really, as I imagine
                                her walking
        a second treacherous tightrope
                                between mothers,
    a tightrope I'm still swaying on.

7. "Fierce, alone, utterly different"

She walked by herself into the biting
        blasts off Lake Michigan, threw off her jacket,
                                inhaled the air
        "like a bug-killing tonic, a freezing
                                acid
        that burns me down to who I really am,
                                fierce,
        alone, utterly different,"
                                she had written
        when she returned from one such outing,
                                shivering,
        exhilarated, with a singed throat
                                that laid her up
through four fateful fortunate weeks,

infected days in bed when the novel
        and the theater revealed themselves to her as
                                her destiny,
        she told her diary, rather grandly,
                        but not
        without prophetic sagacity,
                a
        time when, without distraction, she
                                immersed her self
        in Edna Ferber's *Show Boat* and left
                        a part of
        that self on that boat—as she had done,
                                disembarking,
    unaware, fifteen years before.

8. Her Mother's Moonlit Past

As her fever rose, so did the slow float
        of the Mississippi, the rise of the boat
                                and its soft fall
        coming into Cairo, or Baton Rouge, or
                        Memphis,
        a permanence in impermanence,
                        stops
        along the way, dense with danger,
                        threats natural—
        a quiet summer dusk suddenly
                        imploding
        in an overwhelmingly dark sky,
                        patrons scrambling
    on the gangplank, the river bank

all at once sub-marine, yellow water
        over and under the floating theater—
                                and threats human,
        the urge to escape surging through her
                                as she
        came to the word "miscegenation,"
                                chilled
        by its hiss through the sheriff's teeth,
                                imperiling
        Julie, the Ferber character I
                                believe to be
        sacred to my mother, an exile
                                over water,
of questionable origin.

As Mary's fever rose (she later wrote),
        she felt "a glow, as of the revelation of
                                my history
        and future life, start to surround me on
                                my bed,
        and the more I learned about Julie's
                                fate
        the more she inhabited me, her
                                glittering
        ability on the floating stage,
                                an actress
        'natural and intuitive,' such
                                as, suddenly,
I vowed that I would someday be.

"Julie Dozier's uncertain parentage
          was not unlike my own; our vagabondage—
                              Julie's across
          the South and Upper Midwest, mine spanning
                                        the sea,
          to Chicago, Rogers Park, to who
                              knows
          where? I know it will be far from here."
                                        But
          for now she knew she wanted to be
                              here, sunk
          down into her story at such great
                                        depths that she could,
like a surprised angler snaring

a catch beyond her capabilities,
          find surfacing in her diary writing
                              fine as the books
          she was reading, but writing about *her*
                              hidden
          heart. To expose that life in black and
                              white
          to others in a scandalous memoir,
                              an exposé
          of the perils of an immigrant
                              girl, her rise
          from the streets, etc., would rip
                              open old wounds
intolerably. Hence fiction:

Her Mother's Moonlit Past. That book, her first,
     made Mary, at age 18, an overnight
               literary
     sensation. (*Regarding my own gropings*
               for her,
     he title could equally apply
               to
     a book of my own, this *book*
               I am writing,
     right here, right now.) It came to Mary
               that febrile
     night in the afterglow of *Show Boat*:
               "a vision of
who I will be from here on in."

10. A Glittering Life

The fever broke. She saw her fate. "As I
     lay there on the bedspread, burning up, a life
               seemed to unroll
     from the foot of my bed, a glittering
               life
     on the stage and on the screen. But first
               I
     would have to solve the riddle of
               who my mother
     was—or, rather, who she might have been,
               since I know
     nothing about her." Fiction must do
               when facts are few,
and the very next day, limited

by nothing, she wrote the first three chapters
        of her imaginary mother's life, or
                                her real mother's
        life intuited by her daughter in
                        the womb.
        Mary wrote without ceasing. Mary wrote
                                in
        a flow: "Born in Lvov, under straitened
                                circumstances,
        Gertrude Louise Lichtenstein had,
                        from an early
        age, dreamed of spinning across a stage
                        in a bonnet
and fluted yellow hoop-skirt, twirl-

ing a parasol and turning to you,
        the audience, to play the part of who
                        she really was.
        Yet she was born in rags, and it would be
                        aeons
        before Gertrude stepped forth to pluck the
                                full
        flower of her dream." So began
                        the novel, and
        from it flowed five other epics, all
                        in five years
        time. She was 23 and famous,
                        empurpled in
the public mind, a heroine

herself, promenading through the glossies,
        the glamorous waif who managed to escape
                                the clutches of
        poverty, had run away and written
                                her way
        to a stardom that filled the vacuum
                                of
        the Depression, lit the abyss
                                of the nation's
        longing with a saga exploring
                                the unknown
        origin of the orphan she was,
                                her own makeshift
past in the guise of a mother.

Epilogue

Mary left for Hollywood to become
        Marion Allen, the actress the world came
                                to know her as,
        the star of "Time's Chariot," "Woman
                                of the Wind,"
        "Lustful," and other melodramas
                                through
        the sixties. She contended for
                                six Oscars;
        lost all six; was honored for lifetime
                                achievement.
        Under the wing of her fourth husband
                                she converted
to a creed of political

activism; dedicated herself
        to the elimination of poverty;
                                traveled widely,
        but never on safari, the weight of
                                the poor
        on her mind until the day she died,
                                the
        likely heirs of her legacy—
                                anyone but
        me, your only daughter. Oh Miriam!
                                Oh Mary!
        Oh Marion! I vow to be your
                                biographer.
But mother, I am so bitter.

ABOUT THE AUTHOR

The Biographer is DAVID M. KATZ's fifth book of poetry, preceded by *In Praise of Manhattan*, *Stanzas on Oz*, and *Claims of Home*, all published by Dos Madres Press, and *The Warrior in the Forest*, published by House of Keys Press. Poems of his have appeared in *Poetry*, *The Paris Review*, *The Hudson Review*, *The New Criterion*, *PN Review* (UK), *The New Republic*, *The Hopkins Review*, *Shenandoah*, *Alabama Literary Review*, *The Cortland Review*, and *The Ekphrastic Review*. He is a co-host of the Morningside Poetry Series in Manhattan and posts frequently on his website, The David M. Katz Poetry Blog (davidmkatzpoet.com). He is starring in *Gulliver's Paradise*, a film by Shalom Gorewitz that is currently in production.

Other books by David M. Katz
published by Dos Madres Press

In Praise of Manhattan (2020)
Stanzas on Oz (2015)
Claims of Home (2011)

He is also included in:
Realms of the Mothers:
The First Decade of Dos Madres Press - 2016

For the full Dos Madres Press catalog:
www.dosmadres.com